Making
Decisions

Pocket Mentor Series

The *Pocket Mentor* Series offers immediate solutions to common challenges managers face on the job every day. Each book in the series is packed with handy tools, self-tests, and real-life examples to help you identify your strengths and weaknesses and hone critical skills. Whether you're at your desk, in a meeting, or on the road, these portable guides enable you to tackle the daily demands of your work with greater speed, savvy, and effectiveness.

Books in the series:

Making
Decisions

Expert Solutions to Everyday Challenges

Harvard Business Press

Boston, Massachusetts

No part of this publication may be reproduced, stored in or introduced into a re-
trieval system, or transmitted, in any form, or by any means (electronic, mechanical,
photocopying, recording, or otherwise), without the prior permission of the pub-
lisher. Requests for permission should be directed to permissions@hbsp.harvard.edu,
or mailed to Permissions, Harvard Business School Publishing, 60 Harvard Way,
Boston, Massachusetts 02163.

Library of Congress Cataloging-in-Publication Data

Making decisions : expert solutions to everyday challenges.
     p. cm. — (Pocket mentor series)
  Includes bibliographical references.
  ISBN 978-1-4221-2871-8
  1. Decision making—Handbooks, manuals, etc.
  HD30.23.M342 2008
  153.8'3—dc22

                    2008024143

The paper used in this publication meets the requirements of the American National
Standard for Permanence of Paper for Publications and Documents in Libraries and
Archives Z39.48-1992.

Contents

Tips and Tools   71

Test Yourself   83

A helpful review of concepts presented in this guide. Take it before and after you've read the guide, to see how much you've learned.

Answers to test questions   86

To Learn More   91

Further titles of articles and books if you want to go more deeply into the topic.

Sources for Making Decisions   99

Notes   101

For you to use as ideas come to mind.

Mentor's Message: The Business Value of Making Smart Decisions

Think back on the last critical decision you faced at work. A lot was riding on your choice, yet the best alternative was probably not clear. There were trade-offs to be made. What's more, you knew that the path you chose would have a real impact on your company and its people. How did you feel when making that decision? And afterward? Was your choice a good one?

The higher the stakes in the business world, the more charged the decision-making process becomes. To make the smartest decisions, you need to take the mystery out of the process and make it more of a science. Understanding the eight steps to an effective decision can help. This volume covers each step in detail—from setting the stage for a particular decision and recognizing common obstacles, to generating and evaluating alternatives and communicating the final decision to stakeholders. You'll also find guidelines for assessing your overall decision-making approach, so you can continually strengthen it as you gain experience making business decisions.

David A. Garvin, Mentor

David A. Garvin is the C. Roland Christensen Professor of Business Administration at Harvard Business School, where he specializes in leadership and general management. For more than twenty-five years, he has studied and taught the principles of organizational learning, business and management processes, and the design and leadership of large, complex organizations. He is the author or coauthor of nine books, including *General Management: Processes and Action, Learning in Action, Education for Judgment*, and *Managing Quality*, as well as thirty articles and eight videotape series. He is a three-time winner of the McKinsey Award, given annually for the best article in *Harvard Business Review*.

Making Decisions: The Basics

What Is
Decision Making?

A S A MANAGER, YOU are faced with decisions every day. Some decisions are straightforward, such as deciding which team member to assign to a specific project. Others are more complex, such as selecting a new vendor or deciding to discontinue a product due to weak sales.

Many managers tend to view decision making as an event—a choice to be made at a single point in time, usually by an individual or a small group. In reality, however, significant decisions are seldom made in the moment by one manager or in one meeting. Simply put, decision making is a social or group process that unfolds over time.

"Effective executives know that decision making has its own systemic process and its own clearly defined elements."
—Peter Drucker

Decision making as a group process

Important decisions, such as changing the strategic direction of a group or hiring a new manager, typically require time and input from many individuals and sources of information throughout an organization. Hence, decision making can more accurately be viewed as a *group process*.

Managers who recognize decision making as a group process increase their likelihood of making more effective decisions. Why? By taking time, they are able to identify and assess the issues associated with making the decision. By involving others, they weigh different perspectives and deepen the discussion. Perhaps most important, taking a process-driven approach is more likely to lead to broader acceptance of the decision—which in turn leads to more effective implementation.

Making decisions: eight steps

We can think of the decision-making process as consisting of eight steps:

1. **Setting the stage.** You select participants and determine the approach you will take to reach a decision: will you aim for consensus or vote by majority? During the meetings, especially the earliest ones, you set the tone for the group by encouraging open dialogue and promoting healthy debate.

2. **Recognizing obstacles.** Certain individual biases and group dynamics can be obstacles in the decision-making process. By predicting and recognizing these tendencies, you can take action to avoid them.

3. **Framing the issue.** A successful decision depends on a clear understanding of the issue at hand and its root cause(s).

4. **Generating alternatives.** After you've clarified the issue, you brainstorm and generate creative conflict to develop alternative courses of action and ways of proceeding.

5. **Evaluating alternatives.** Next, you assess the feasibility, risk, and ethical implications of each possible course of action.

6. **Making a decision.** You choose an alternative.

7. **Communicating the decision.** You decide who should be notified of your decision, and communicate it effectively.

8. **Implementing the decision.** You determine what tasks will be required to put the decision into action, assign resources, and establish deadlines.

Throughout this eight-step process, you also continually assess your decision-making effectiveness and make changes as needed to improve it.

In the sections that follow, we'll take a closer look at each of the eight steps in the decision-making process. Then we'll examine ways to assess the effectiveness of your process.

Step 1: Setting the Stage

S ETTING THE STAGE for the decision-making process is critical to making successful choices. This step consists of:

- Selecting the right people to participate in the process

- Choosing an approach for making the actual decision

- Creating a climate that promotes healthy debate and allows for diverse viewpoints

Let's take a closer look at each of these three tasks.

Determining who will participate in the decision

A group of people with diverse perspectives is more likely to generate a variety of thoughtful ideas about how to make a particular decision than a group of individuals with the same background. When you choose people for your decision-making group, look for individuals who are likely to express differing points of view and who represent different interests. Your group should include:

- **Key stakeholders.** These are the people who will be most directly affected by the decision or who have a stake in the decision. You need their buy-in to put the decision into effect. Since they are more likely to support a decision they helped make, include them early in the process to ensure an efficient implementation.

- **Experts.** Experts can educate the group and provide information about the feasibility of various courses of action you're considering. Keep in mind that you may need more than one area of expertise represented in your group.

- **Opponents.** If you are aware of individuals who may oppose the decision and block its implementation, invite them to one or more of your meetings. Involving potential opponents early on can eliminate obstacles down the road.

Ideally, your group should be small in size, preferably between five and seven members. Depending on the complexity of the decision at hand, you may want to involve as many as ten or as few as two people in the decision-making process.

Selecting a decision-making approach

Once you've selected the participants, determine what decision-making approach you will take. The group you assemble needs to understand up front the process it will follow and how the final decision will be made. The spectrum of group decision-making approaches includes four general types:

- **Consensus.** All team members meet together to discuss the proposal openly and strive to reach agreement, with everyone accepting the final decision.

What Would YOU Do?

Keeping Up with the Joneses

ESLIE IS A TECHNICAL manager at Smith Enterprises, an industrial-quality tool manufacturing company. The products that she and her engineers develop are manufactured internally. Leslie knows the manufacturing department is overburdened and frequently delivers its products late, resulting in delayed shipments to customers. She's noticed that Smith Enterprises' main competitor—Jones Tool, Inc.—as well as several additional rival firms, is developing products faster by outsourcing the manufacturing process. In light of this, she's afraid that her company will lose new business. Leslie's boss has asked her to investigate outsourcing options and decide how they should proceed. She thinks the answer is clear—manufacturing the products externally would save significant amounts of time and money. Leslie senses that her boss is in favor of this option as well. She is inclined to personally gather the information that supports outsourcing and submit a proposal to her boss immediately but wonders whether that would be the best first step.

What would YOU do? The mentor will suggest a solution in *What You COULD Do*.

- **Majority.** The group votes and the majority rules. The team leader may elect to break a tie, if necessary.

- **Qualified consensus.** The team tries to reach a collective agreement, but if it is unable to do so, the team agrees that the team leader makes the decision.

- **Directive leadership.** The leader makes the decision and then informs the group of the decision that was made. A crisis or sudden unexpected emergency is a classic example of when this approach might be necessary.

These approaches, with the exception of directive leadership, vary in the extent that they empower the participants and create a sense of responsibility within the group. Be aware, however, that regardless of approach, when a group is trying to find areas of agreement, it may avoid exploring minority viewpoints. Your job as a manager is to encourage exploration of all ideas, no matter what approach you will take to make the decision.

Fostering the right climate

To help your group generate creative solutions to problems and evaluate them critically, choose diverse settings for your meetings. Such settings might include conference rooms that you don't typically work in, off-site locations, or a familiar location with the furniture rearranged to facilitate face-to-face discussion. When people are removed from traditional settings, such as a boardroom or a supervisor's office, they tend to speak more freely because they feel less constrained by office hierarchies.

You'll also need to create a consistent climate, or tone, for your decision-making meetings. The climate you establish strongly influences how members of your team interact with one another.

Consider the following scenario: A manager at a software development company has been charged with assigning limited resources to the firm's current projects. The manager calls a meeting with all of her project leaders to discuss how the resources will be allocated. The discussion quickly turns into an argument. Each project leader advocates for his or her project. The debate gets heated as the conversation goes around in circles, and each project leader disparages the others' efforts. Ultimately, the manager decides to assign the limited resources to three projects. The project leaders leave the meeting exhausted and frustrated.

What went wrong? The manager did not manage the decision-making process effectively, and the meeting deteriorated into an *advocacy* mode. The project leaders viewed the meeting as a competition. They advocated for their positions without considering the needs of other departments or the company as a whole. In advocacy situations, people tend to offer only the information that supports their case and omit details that might weaken it. As a result, the discussion can quickly deteriorate into personal attacks, giving rise to negative emotions.

In a perfect world, decisions would be made using an *inquiry* approach—an open process in which individuals ask probing questions, explore different points of view, and identify a wide range of options with the goal of reaching a decision that the group creates and owns collectively. In an inquiry mode, individuals set aside their personal opinions or preferences in order to arrive at a decision that is best for the group or organization.

The table "Approaches to decision making" illustrates the advocacy approach versus the inquiry approach to decision making.

While inquiry is an ideal, it is seldom met in practice. It is extremely difficult for individuals to discuss ideas or issues without expressing their opinions. A more realistic and effective technique for arriving at a decision is one that *balances* advocacy with inquiry. Group members leave their personal agendas behind and enter the

Approaches to decision making

	Advocacy	Inquiry
Concept of decision making	A contest	Collaborative problem solving
Purpose of discussion	Persuasion and lobbying	Testing and evaluation
Participants' role	Spokespeople	Critical thinkers
Patterns of behavior	• Strive to persuade others • Defend your position • Downplay weaknesses	• Present balanced arguments • Remain open to alternatives • Accept constructive criticism
Minority views	Discouraged or dismissed	Cultivated and valued
The outcome	Winners and losers	Collective ownership

meeting with the intention of acting as unbiased participants. They may advocate for a position they feel strongly about, but they also inquire into other viewpoints and consider alternatives. They understand that the goal is to find the best solution for the group as a whole, even if it means that some individuals in the group might be negatively affected by the decision. Generally, in sessions that balance advocacy with inquiry, people share information freely and consider multiple alternatives.

What You COULD Do.

Remember Leslie's dilemma about how to initially approach the outsourcing decision?

Here's what the mentor suggests:

What may seem like a clear answer to Leslie may not be the best approach to arriving at the best business decision. In order for Leslie to make the best decision, she needs to assemble a group that first will concentrate on understanding why Smith Enterprises' current process is costly and inefficient and then will explore possible alternatives for improving the process. The group should consist of engineers as well as people outside her department—for example, someone from manufacturing and possibly sales. Including people with diverse backgrounds and areas of expertise will help Leslie make a more informed decision. Once the team identifies the underlying reasons for the issue they are facing, they should then generate and evaluate a number of alternatives for resolving the issue. Although Leslie's inclination is to solve the problem a certain way, she should look for information and evaluate options that support alternative solutions. By involving others and evaluating a wide range of options, Leslie will increase her chances of making a successful decision.

Step 2: Recognizing Obstacles

D ECISION MAKING IS made difficult by common, often unconscious, obstacles that frequently inhibit a decision maker's ability to determine the optimal choice. Such obstacles include cognitive biases and unproductive group dynamics. While it is almost impossible to eliminate these obstacles, recognizing them in yourself and in the members of your group will help you make more objective decisions.

Anticipating cognitive biases

Here are some common examples of cognitive biases—distortions or preconceived notions—that people encounter when making decisions.

- Bias toward the familiar and toward past successes. We tend to base our decisions on events and information that are familiar to us. For example, Susan, a brand manager, remembers her launch of a new product in Spain three years ago; it was her first big marketing success. She also vaguely remembers that a similar launch strategy was *un*successful in a number of other countries. Because her memories of the successful Spanish launch are so vivid, she emphasizes this experience and discounts the evidence of unsuccessful launches elsewhere. When Susan tries to extend a new brand into Portugal, her efforts fail. While the strategy used for the Spanish launch may have been a good starting point, her reliance on a prior success led to incorrect assumptions about the Portuguese market.

- **Bias toward accepting assumptions at face value.** We are generally overconfident in our assumptions and therefore generate too few alternatives. For instance, Brock purchases a software package offered by the largest vendor without collecting competitive bids. He assumes that because the package works for other users in the same industry, it will work for him. He fails to investigate other software packages that might better meet his needs.

- **Bias toward the status quo.** We have a tendency to resist major deviations from the status quo. For example, managers at BigCo are familiar with how to use a particular computer program and resist using an alternative, even though their program is outdated. Their resistance is driven more by their reluctance to learn something new than by the quality of the system itself.

- **Bias toward confirming our opinion.** Once we form an opinion, we typically seek out information that supports our viewpoint and ignore facts that may challenge it. For example, Dinah searches the Internet to find data supporting her preference for focus groups in market research, but she does not stop to read information that supports other approaches.

COGNITIVE BIAS *n* 1: a systematic error introduced into sampling or testing by selecting or encouraging one outcome or answer over others

How do you prevent these biases from adversely affecting your decision-making ability? The best way is to recognize them, by ensuring that contrarian, diverse voices get introduced into the discussion.

"We tend to subconsciously decide what to do before figuring out why we want to do it."
—John S. Hammond, Ralph L. Keeney, and Howard Raiffa

Managing group dynamics

One of the advantages to treating decision making as a group process is that individual biases can be counteracted by the presence of multiple voices and perspectives.

But while groups offer different viewpoints, they need guidance to be productive. Your challenge is to *manage* the group decision-making process. Otherwise, you may find yourself confronted with one of the following extremes.

- **Excessive group harmony.** Excessive group harmony occurs when individuals want to be accepted in a group or they lack interest in the process. When people strive too hard to be accepted in the group, they may fall victim to *groupthink*. With groupthink, participants' desire for agreement overrides their motivation to evaluate alternative options. In this situation, people tend to withhold their opinions, especially if their views differ from those of the group leader. They make little effort to obtain new information from experts, and they selectively filter information to support their initial preferences. They may spend a lot of time inquiring about what others in the group want so that the solution they reach will make everyone happy.

Excessive group harmony can also stem from lack of interest: participants have no interest in the process or do not feel empowered. If the group feels that the leader has already made the decision, they may go along with it, refuse to participate entirely, or accept the first reasonable alternative that is proposed in an effort to end the process.

- **Excessive individualism.** Excessive individualism is at the opposite end of the spectrum from excessive group harmony. In this situation, individuals engage in aggressive advocacy, placing stakes in the ground and relentlessly arguing their positions. They disregard the opinions of other group members and fail to consider the common good.

Either of these extreme behaviors can lengthen the decision-making process and interfere with the team's effort to make good choices. Your job as a manager is to keep your decision-making group on track so it does not head toward either of these extremes.

Step 3: Framing the Issue at Hand

ONCE YOU'VE SET the stage and recognized common obstacles that can stand in the way of decision making, you're ready to frame the issue for your decision-making team. A key task during this step is to avoid the common error of seeking out solutions before you understand the nature (the root cause) of the issue at hand.

Distinguishing between symptoms and root causes

Consider the following story: New Age Electronics, a toy manufacturer, has a support phone line to answer customers' questions about assembling its products. The volume of phone calls has increased so much that the phone-support associates can't keep up with the demand. Customers have complained about waiting as long as half an hour to get help. Tai, the manager responsible for the support line, puts together a team to help him decide how to address the issue. He begins the first meeting by saying, "We have a serious problem with our customer support line. Customers are waiting too long for service. We need to fix it."

Because Tai has framed the issue as a problem with the phone-line response time, the team is most likely to focus on ways to reduce the response time—for example, adding more phone lines, adding more phone representatives, or increasing the hours of service. These solutions will address the *symptoms* of the problem—overloaded phone lines—but may not address the *root* of the problem.

Tip: When you're having a difficult time understanding the problem, consider moving to a new setting as this might trigger new insights.

To get to the root of the problem, Tai's team should be thinking about *why* customer calls have increased dramatically. Is one product in particular responsible for an inordinate number of calls? Is there a flaw in the design of a product or in the assembly instructions? Are the phone-support associates poorly trained? Suppose Tai had framed the issue by saying, "We have a serious problem with our customer support line. The volume of calls has increased, customers are waiting too long for service, and we need to find out why. Then we need to decide what to do about it." This framing would better guide the team toward uncovering the root cause of the problem. The team would thus stand a better chance of eventually deciding on a course of action that would address the cause of the problem instead of just treating a symptom of the problem.

Performing a root-cause analysis

To ensure that you get to the core of a problem, perform a root-cause analysis. During this process, you repeatedly make a statement of fact and ask the question *why*.

For example, Carla, the general manager of a pizza parlor, noticed that she was losing sales because her home deliveries were slower than her competitor's. Her friend suggests that they invest in a fleet of delivery vehicles to solve this problem. Instead of jumping to this conclusion, Carla asks, "Our pizza deliveries are slow. Why? Our delivery associates drive old cars that are in poor condition. Why? They can't afford repairs or newer cars. Why? They don't have the money. Why? Their pay is too low." Through this process, she realizes that the older, poorly maintained vehicles are a symptom of lower wages than those competitors paid.

Tip: When looking for the cause of a problem, look for something that changed at the same time the problem arose—you'll often find the cause there.

Root-cause analysis can work well for an individual, a small group, or in brainstorming sessions.

A tool that can help you perform such an analysis is called a *fishbone diagram*. As the figure, "Fishbone diagram" demonstrates, every fishbone diagram will look a little different, depending on the particular problem being solved.

When confronted with a problem, think about how to frame the issue for your team. Be careful not to assume from the outset that you know what the problem is. Challenge yourself and your team to get at the core of the issue by framing the problem in a variety of different ways and assessing whether the available infor-

Fishbone diagram

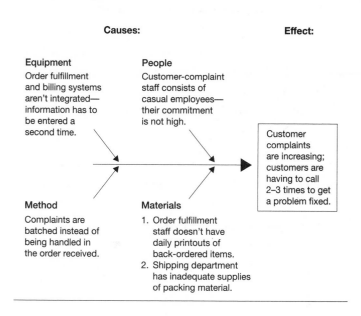

Causes:

Effect:

Equipment
Order fulfillment and billing systems aren't integrated—information has to be entered a second time.

People
Customer-complaint staff consists of casual employees—their commitment is not high.

Customer complaints are increasing; customers are having to call 2–3 times to get a problem fixed.

Method
Complaints are batched instead of being handled in the order received.

Materials
1. Order fulfillment staff doesn't have daily printouts of back-ordered items.
2. Shipping department has inadequate supplies of packing material.

mation supports your theories. Throughout the entire process, ask *why* and other open-ended questions (those not requiring simply a yes or no response). Such questions encourage exploration more than closed questions based on predefined assumptions about the problem or requiring a yes or no response.

"If you have a 'yes man' working for you, one of you is redundant."
   —Barry Rand, former CEO, Avis

Articulating your
decision-making objectives

Once you have successfully framed the issue at hand, identify your objectives in determining a course of action. Ask your team questions like "What do you want the decision we make to accomplish?" and "What would you like to see happen as a result of the decision we reach?" Invite group members to describe their vision of the outcome of the decision as vividly and specifically as possible.

For example, if you were the manager at New Age Electronics, you and your team might come up with the following objectives:

- Reduce the average waiting time per customer to two minutes.

- Reduce call volume by 40 percent.

- Reduce average call duration to three minutes.

During the objective-setting process, you may encounter significant differences in opinion from one person to another. This is a healthy part of the dialogue and should be encouraged. However, if you find your list of objectives spiraling out of control, you may want to revisit the issue you're trying to address. You may find that you have more than one issue to resolve.

Once you have created a list of objectives, it's time to think about the possible courses of action you may take to achieve those goals.

1. **Specify the objectives you want to reach.**

   What are you trying to achieve by making a decision? Make sure that as many people as possible with a stake in solving the problem are asked to specify their objectives. If you find you're hearing two or more substantially different objectives, you may conclude you're actually facing two or more problems, or that more than a few stakeholders don't understand the problem, or that different groups hope to see the problem solved in very different ways.

2. **Define—as specifically as possible—the performance level that represents a successful outcome.**

   Do you want a solution that boosts sales? By what percentage? For all regions? Be as precise as you can be.

3. **"Paint" a picture of what things will look like when the problem is solved.**

   Invite all stakeholders to describe the desired future state in as much detail as possible. Let imaginations and creativity run loose. Here, too, you may find significant divergence from one person to another. You may resolve differences by compromise, by straight selection of one view over another, or by determining that you in fact have two or more problems at hand.

4. **Make sure your agreed-on objectives and outcomes are not in conflict.**

   You may have determined that part of your solution to customer complaints about telephone orders is to have all of your phone-order reps take an additional three weeks of training. Another part of the solution is to reduce standards for each rep's completed orders per hour from eight to seven. But can you have the lower staffing levels due to training and the fewer customers handled by each rep at the same time? Will customers then complain more about long waits to have their orders taken? If yes, goals may have to be adjusted.

Step 4: Generating Alternatives

T O MAKE AN INFORMED decision, you need choices—alternative courses of action you might take to resolve the issue at hand. Generating alternatives creates those choices. After weighing the merits of a variety of options, you are in a better position to make the best decision for the situation facing you. Here, it's important to recognize that a "go/no-go" choice does not mean you have generated multiple alternatives—go/no-go is only a single option.

Consider the following story:

Paul, a marketing manager at a consumer products company, calls a meeting with his team to discuss how to increase laundry detergent sales in Latin America. The meeting begins with silence as everyone waits for someone else to speak. Paul breaks the silence by suggesting they consider changing the current packaging. Following this cue, someone chimes in with supporting statistics about packaging and consumer trends. Another person then describes the packaging of a product that has done well in Latin America. The meeting concludes with the assignment of a task force to research new packaging options.

This meeting seemed to proceed smoothly. But something's wrong. Paul didn't engage the team in generating alternatives. He didn't promote healthy debate or constructive conflict. Instead, excessive group harmony resulted in an action step based on the first idea that emerged: investigate packaging options. There was little creativity or innovative thinking. As a result, no *new* ideas surfaced. The group settled on the first alternative suggested, which had been Paul's idea!

Paul could have helped his group generate a wider range of promising alternatives if he had applied certain practices, such as brainstorming, dialoguing, and promoting fair process.

Brainstorming

Brainstorming is an effective way to generate different ideas and courses of action. How do you brainstorm? Start with a blank flip chart page. At the start of a meeting, ask your team members to suggest any ideas that come into their heads. Or ask individuals to take a few minutes to develop their own lists of ideas to share publicly.

Either way, record the ideas but don't discuss their merits at this point. Be especially careful not to allow criticism in the early stages. Instead, focus on identifying as many alternatives as possible. You can evaluate the ideas *after* you have a list of possibilities.

Tip: Before brainstorming, write the problem, issue, or question the group will brainstorm on a chalkboard or flip chart, where everyone can see it throughout the session. Get agreement from everyone that the issue is stated correctly and precisely.

Encouraging productive dialogue

Energize your team so that they will work hard to identify creative solutions. Creative conflict is essential to the generation of alternatives, but it should never be personal or divisive. Promote team participation during your brainstorming sessions by employing the following tactics:

- Encourage open, candid dialogue by making it clear at the outset that the final outcome is not predetermined and that everyone's input will be valued.

- Suggest that people try to think outside of their individual or departmental roles. They should focus on what's best for the group, using all of the available information.

- Provide closure at the end of every meeting by assigning tasks and deadlines so people are accountable for moving the process forward.

- Recognize and thank people who share their ideas and viewpoints in a positive manner—especially those who are willing to take the risk of challenging you.

Tip: Ask team members to play devil's advocate by researching and making a case against their preferred proposal. Ask them to explain in detail why the preferred option should *not* be adopted.

Promoting fair process

Throughout the decision-making process, it is essential that your team members feel that the process is fair. Specifically, they must believe that their ideas were acknowledged and considered, even if their suggestions were not ultimately adopted. This sense of fairness is critical for ensuring cooperation and buy-in when it comes time to implement the group's decision.

Alternatives provide the choices you will need to make an informed decision. When you encourage team participation, facilitate creative conflict, and listen to ideas, you are likely to generate a full slate of options that will serve you well as you enter the next step in the decision-making process: evaluating the alternatives your group has generated.

Tip: Either take notes yourself or appoint a note taker to show that you are considering everyone's ideas and that their input is valued and respected.

Step 5: Evaluating Alternatives

ONCE YOUR GROUP HAS generated alternatives to consider, it's time to evaluate those alternatives and select one as the final decision. How to pick the best solution? Your group can weigh a range of variables as well as use one or more systematic methods for reaching a decision: the prioritization matrix, the trade-off technique, or the decision tree.

Weighing a range of variables

To evaluate the alternatives your group has generated, members can take stock of how well each alternative meets the objectives you established at the outset of the decision-making process. The table "Variables for evaluating an alternative" shows examples.

Variables for evaluating an alternative

Variable	Questions to ask
Costs	• How much will this alternative cost? • Will it result in a cost savings now or over the long term? • Are there any hidden costs? • Are there likely to be additional costs down the road? • Does this alternative meet budget constraints?
Benefits	• What kind of profits will we realize if we implement this alternative? • Will it increase the quality of our product? • Will customer satisfaction increase?

Variable	Questions to ask
Intangibles	• Will our reputation improve if we implement this alternative? • Will our customers and/or our employees be more loyal?
Time	• How long will it take to implement this alternative? • Could there be delays? If so, what impact will this have on any schedules?
Feasibility	• Can this alternative be implemented realistically? • Are there any obstacles that must be overcome? • If this alternative is implemented, what resistance might be encountered inside or outside the organization?
Resources	• How many people are needed to implement this alternative? • Are they available? • What other projects will suffer if individuals focus on this option?
Risks	• What are the risks associated with this alternative? • Could this option result in loss of profits or competitive advantage? • Will competitors respond? If so, how?
Ethics	• Is this alternative legal? • Is it in the best interests of the customers, the employees, and the community where we operate? • Would I feel comfortable if other people knew about this alternative?

Using a prioritization matrix

Another method for evaluating alternatives is to create a prioritization matrix. To create the matrix:

1. List your objectives for making the decision at hand.

2. Assign each objective a value (highest = best).

3. Make each objective, along with its corresponding value, a column header for your matrix.

4. Make each alternative a row.

5. For each alternative, rate the objectives on a scale of 1 to 10 (10 = best).

6. Multiply your ratings by the priority values.

7. Add all the scores for each alternative to determine which has the highest number. This is your best decision, based on your priorities.

The table "Sample prioritization matrix" shows an example of how one group filled out a prioritization matrix.

Analyzing trade-offs

Like a prioritization matrix, a trade-off table can help you evaluate the various alternatives you've generated for the decision. The table "Sample trade-off table," shown on page 42, displays an example.

Sample prioritization matrix

	Increase profits (4)	Maintain low customer costs (3)	Implement quickly (2)	Use few internal resources (1)	Total score
Alternative A	9 * 4 = 36	2 * 3 = 6	7 * 2 = 14	2 * 1 = 2	58
Alternative B	2 * 4 = 8	9 * 3 = 27	8 * 2 = 16	3 * 1 = 3	54

What Would YOU Do?

Is That *Really* the Way the Cookie Crumbles?

LYLE IS A BRAND manager at a consumer products company, currently managing a gourmet cookie product. Sales of the cookie have been flat for the past eighteen months. Marketing studies have shown that only a limited number of consumers are willing to pay a premium price for a box of cookies, regardless of the quality. Lyle is faced with the challenge of increasing sales without diluting his brand's image. Senior management has made it clear that Lyle needs to find a solution fast.

Lyle assembles a group of five people to identify ways to increase revenues without diluting the cookie brand's image. The group has a mix of people with different backgrounds and levels of expertise. Three of the participants are from his staff, one is from sales, and the other is from research and development. The group explores options ranging from initiating a coupon program to reducing prices to forging corporate partnerships. After thorough discussion and analysis, the team decides that forming a partnership with another company is the most promising option.

Lyle identifies several ice cream companies as potential partners for creating a new (and hopefully best-selling) product: an ice cream sandwich with whimsical images of animals printed on the cookie portions of the confection. While he's in the early stages of researching these companies, Supreme Ice Cream approaches him about a partnership. Supreme is eager to move forward and is offering what appear to be very attractive terms for the deal. Lyle mulls over his next move. Should he grab the opportunity to partner with Supreme? Revisit the decision that a partnership is the best option for increasing revenues? Seek out other offers and then evaluate the Supreme deal? The whole thing has begun to feel as opaque as a bowl of cookie batter.

What would YOU do? The mentor will suggest a solution in *What You COULD Do.*

Sample trade-off table

	Profits	Customer costs	Time to implement	Internal resources
Alternative A	Profits increase by $100,000	Cost to customer increases by $1 per unit	6 months to implement	20 people required
Alternative B	Profits increase by $10,000	Cost to customer increases by $0	4 months to implement	15 people required

Once you lay out the alternatives with their associated information, consider how important these factors are to your group and/or the company, and identify the compromises that you are willing to make.

For example, would a $90,000 increase in profits be worth the time of five extra people?

Be sure to think about the trade-offs in light of the priority you assign to each objective.

Using a decision tree

Decision trees are another form of systematic approach to evaluating alternatives. Consider a situation in which you project an increased demand for your product. You and your team need to decide whether to continue manufacturing a component internally or whether to outsource the work. The figure, "Decision tree," shown on the next page presents a simplified view of your alternatives.

According to this simplified decision tree, the best course of action would be to pursue alternative B. (Of the two options, alternative B offers the highest risk-adjusted net present value.)

"When you come to a fork in the road, take it."
—Yogi Berra

Decision trees are typically much more robust than the one in the previous figure in that they evaluate more options and include

Decision tree

Alternative A
Keep the work in-house. Cost per unit remains the same, but the number of products developed is limited. No jobs are eliminated.

Demand increases. Research suggests probability is 80%.

Your company can't keep up with orders and may lose business to competitors. Prices remain the same. The net present value of expected change to profits, including investment costs, is –$1M.

Demand decreases. Research suggests probability is 20%.

Your company is able to fulfill orders and keep costs low. The net present value of expected change to profits, including investment costs, is –$0.

Alternative B
Outsource the work. Cost per unit increases, but more products can be developed. Manufacturing jobs are eliminated.

Demand increases. Research suggests probability is 50%.

You are able to meet the demand and sell more products. You may or may not have to raise prices to cover your additional costs. The net present value of expected change to profits, including investment costs, is $500K.

Demand decreases. Research suggests probability is 50%.

You have to raise prices to cover additional costs to make less from each sale. Sales stay flat. The net present value of expected change to profits, including investment costs, is –$500K.

◇ Decision point

○ Uncertain event

multiple decision points. In general, the more alternatives you consider, and the more detailed a decision tree you can create, the more likely you are to discover a solution that meets your needs. However, a decision tree won't automatically indicate the best course of action—you'll still need to assess the information in the decision tree to make the wisest choice.

Tip: Encourage constructive contention by inviting others to challenge your opinions and ideas: "My perspective on this is _____; however, I may be wrong. Could you identify any gaps in my logic so we can come up with the most effective decision?"

What You COULD Do.

Remember Lyle's uncertainty about how to respond to Supreme Ice Cream's offer of a partnership deal?

Here's what the mentor suggests:

While it might be tempting to move ahead and establish a partnership immediately with Supreme, it is too early for Lyle to do so at this time. Lyle should wait until other offers have been submitted and evaluate the Supreme Ice Cream offer in relation to those offers. Also, Lyle shouldn't reconvene his group to revisit the decision that a partnership is the best option for increasing revenues. The group has already made its decision. If Lyle reopens the discussion, he runs the risk of taking too much time and missing an opportunity to partner with Supreme Ice Cream. Rehashing old decisions often results in stalled efforts to move forward.

Lyle and his group should pursue other offers and compare them with Supreme Ice Cream's proposal. Evaluating multiple offers will give them a better context in which to make a choice. After careful review, Lyle and his group might realize that Supreme Ice Cream's offer was not as attractive as they originally thought.

Step 6: Making the Decision

I N A PERFECT WORLD, you would have all of the information you need and an unlimited amount of time to make a decision. Your choices would be clear, and company politics would not influence your decision. Often, however, you need to make complex decisions quickly, with only partial information. The techniques for evaluating the alternatives outlined in the previous section should help you compare the pros and cons of each choice. But what if your group is still having difficulty arriving at a final decision—and the clock is ticking? The following suggestions can help.

Moving toward closure

If your group is having difficulty reaching a final decision, consider using the following methods to help the team move toward resolution:

- **Point-counterpoint.** Divide your team into two groups of equal size: group A and group B. Wherever possible, spread supporters of opposing ideas between the groups. Ask group A to develop a proposal for a solution that includes their recommendations and key assumptions. Then have them present their proposal to group B. Then ask group B to identify one or more alternative plans of action and present those plans to group A. Have both groups debate the different proposals until they all agree on a set of recommendations.

For example, a finance department has been engaged in a heated debate over which accounting firm to use to audit the books this year. One group favors a big-name brand, while the other favors a smaller yet well-respected firm. Using the point-counterpoint technique, the decision-making team considers each firm and reaches a conclusion.

- **Intellectual watchdog.** Divide your team into two groups of equal size. Group A develops a proposal for a solution that includes their recommendations and key assumptions. They then present their proposal to group B. Instead of having group B generate an alternative plan of action, ask group B to critique the proposal and present its analysis to group A. Ask group A to revise the proposal on the basis of group B's feedback and present it again. The two groups continue to critique and revise the proposal until they agree on a set of recommendations.

    For example, a manufacturer of office furniture needs to improve the quality of its products. The first group assumes that the problem with quality is due to outdated manufacturing equipment, and recommends investment in better equipment. The second group questions this assumption, critiques the proposal, and presents its analysis to the first group. The first group revises its proposal. The two groups work together in the revision-critique-revision cycle until they arrive at a solution that both groups think will improve their products' quality.

Here are some additional suggestions for resolving disagreements and moving your group toward closure:

- Revisit and retest the assumptions about the issue at hand.

- Go back to the original decision-making objectives and ensure that they are still appropriate.

- Set a deadline for coming to closure—for example, "By next Tuesday, we will make our decision, no matter how much uncertainty remains."

- Agree that if disagreements remain unresolved, the final choice will be made by a particular rule, such as majority voting, group consensus, or a decision by the senior-most member of the group.

Ending the deliberations

Knowing when to end deliberations can be difficult. If a group makes a decision too early, it might not explore enough possibilities. If you sense that your group is rushing to make a decision, consider adjourning a meeting before making a final choice, and reconvening at a later time. Ask each participant to try to find a flaw with the decision to present at the next meeting.

The flip side of deciding too early is deciding too late, which is equally problematic. If the group takes too long to make a decision, it may waste valuable time and possibly even miss the opportunity to solve the problem at hand. If your team insists on hearing every viewpoint and resolving every question before reaching a conclusion, the result is the same: your discussions will become a tiring, endless loop. If you find your group is stuck going around in circles, it is your job as a manager to bring the discussion to closure. You may need to simply "force the issue" by establishing a deadline for a decision, urging your group to use the best information available within that time frame.

Step 7: Communicating the Decision

MANY MANAGERS OVERLOOK one of the most important steps in the decision-making process: communicating the decision to everyone who was involved in it and who will be affected by it. To communicate a decision effectively, you need to take the right approach and make sure you include all the right information in your messages about the decision.

Taking the right approach

Once your group has made a final choice, some members will have to give up their preferred solution. The fairness of the decision-making process as perceived by the participants and others will determine their willingness to support the final outcome. In communicating the decision and getting buy-in for its implementation, keep in mind the following principles:

- **Consideration and voice.** Participants who are encouraged to question and debate each other's ideas are more likely to believe that the leader listened to their viewpoints and gave them serious consideration. This is especially true if you, the leader, have demonstrated attentiveness through your actions—for example, by taking notes and playing back or paraphrasing what was said to show that you were actively listening. Even if some participants' viewpoints did not prevail, knowing that you took them seriously will lend credibility to the process and help everyone to accept the final decision.

- **Explanation.** You need to explain the thinking behind the final decision. It's important to be clear about why you and your group made *this* choice, as opposed to a different one. Explaining the reasons for the decision builds trust in your intentions and confidence that the final choice was made for the benefit of the company as a whole.

- **Expectation.** Once the decision has been made, everyone affected by the decision needs to understand the new rules of the game. Spell out new responsibilities as well as performance measures and penalties for failure to follow the decision. When people clearly understand what's expected of them after a decision has been made, they can focus on what they need to do to support the decision.

The people you notify will include everyone who is responsible for implementing the decision as well as anyone who will be affected by it. Your list might also include other key stakeholders: members of your unit who were not part of the decision-making group, senior management, department supervisors, external constituents, and even customers if they will see a change in the way your company does business with them as a result of the decision.

Including the right content in your message

Your messages about the decision should include the following components:

- Statement of the issue that needed to be addressed

- Description of the objectives or decision-making criteria

- The names and roles of the people involved in making the decision and why they were included in the process

- The alternatives considered (and possibly a summary of the evaluation in table form)

- An explanation of the final decision and what it means for the key stakeholders

- The implementation plan and time frame

- Recognition of those who participated

- Solicitation of feedback

Be sure to take the time to create a clear, concise message. Incomplete or poorly articulated messages about your group's decision can lead to confusion, disappointment, and unwillingness to support its implementation on the part of everyone who hears or reads your messages.

Step 8: Implementing the Decision

YOUR GROUP HAS MADE a choice, and you've communicated the decision to the appropriate people. Now it's time to identify the tasks that will be required to put the decision into action, assign resources, and establish deadlines. Ideally, your team members will leave the final meeting knowing exactly what they're expected to do. If not, reconvene the group to identify who will be responsible for each task.

Assigning tasks, allocating resources

You probably have much of the information you need to develop the plan for implementing your group's decision. When you were evaluating alternatives, you likely considered the cost, the number of people required to work on the project, and so forth.

For example, suppose you and your group have determined that customer complaints about your telephone support line are due to inadequate training of the support associates taking calls. After analyzing the situation, you may decide that the associates need to have more product knowledge. As part of evaluating this alternative, you probably would have identified the resource requirements from the training department to implement your solution.

But be sure to assign reasonable tasks with sufficient resources. For example, the people in the training department may not have extensive product knowledge and may need the help of a content expert. You might need to assign an expert in product knowledge to work with the training department to develop a program.

Monitoring and following up

As you implement your decision, keep track of how things are going. The following practices can help:

- **Clarify expectations and acknowledge incentives.** For example, if an account executive is going to start managing the company's largest client, explain what this client means to the organization and your expectations for managing the relationship. Determine whether the increase in responsibility should result in a pay increase or change in title, and follow up with your human resource department to make that happen.

- **Provide feedback on the implementation.** Give your employees feedback on the progress of the implementation plan. Your input should be constructive and focused on accountability and execution. Set a time for daily or weekly status meetings. This will help you stay informed of your group's progress during implementation.

- **Take a look for yourself.** Check in with people informally. Ask them how the project is going and whether they have any concerns about it. Be interested in not only issues related to implementation, such as schedule and budget, but also whether your employees believe that the project is effectively addressing the problem it is intended to solve.

- **Recognize people's contributions.** Implementation often goes unnoticed unless it fails. If things are going well, recognize individual contributions and celebrate successes.

Keeping abreast of progress during implementation will enable you to fix problems before they become major crises.

Making needed adjustments

Most implementation plans require some adjustment. If nothing else, conditions change over time. So occasional adjustments, ranging from fine-tuning to wholesale changes, are often needed.

What if the decision you've implemented ultimately doesn't work out as you'd expected? In most cases, corrections can be made. These will often involve only "tweaking" the decision you've implemented. But sometimes you may find that the alternative you chose just isn't working. In such cases, you need to revisit the decision-making process.

- Make sure you framed the issue correctly. Have you learned anything new that makes you think the problem is different from what you thought the first time around?

- Has there been a change in your objectives? Do you have new information that you didn't have before? Perhaps you see that one objective should have been given more weight and another one less.

- Have you learned about an alternative that wasn't considered the first time around? Or have you acquired a different perspective that causes you to reassess data you've had for some time?

- Go through your decision-making process again, preferably without reviewing your earlier results. With experience in implementing one alternative, chances are good you'll change your opinion of how well some of the other alternatives satisfy your objectives.

After you've evaluated how well each alternative would be expected to address each objective, return to the results of your first evaluation. Where you find discrepancies between the first time and this time, decide which one is more on target in light of what you know now.

Assessing Your Decision-Making Process

MANY MANAGERS WAIT TO evaluate a decision until the end of the process, after it has been implemented. This is too late. If there is a flaw in the decision itself or in its implementation, you may learn a useful lesson about how *not* to make or implement a decision, but it will be too late to repair the damage.

Assessing the decision-making process is an ongoing effort that must occur in real time, throughout all the phases of the process. For example, you need to monitor the tone of your meetings and address problems in group dynamics *before* they interfere with your goal. Sometimes new information becomes available or new conditions arise, necessitating a midcourse correction in your objectives.

Have a plan for evaluating the various elements in your process, from gathering your decision-making team to implementing the actual decision. It could be something as simple as a checklist. Take the time after each meeting to think about how it went. In addition, understand the distinguishing characteristics of effective decision making.

Understanding the five characteristics of effective decision making

Research suggests decisions that include these five process characteristics have sharply improved the odds of being successful:

- **Multiple alternatives.** Generally, successful decisions result from a review of many alternative solutions. As your process unfolds, make sure that your group considers several alternatives before making its decision. The point-counterpoint approach is a useful method to ensure that at least two alternatives are considered. Remember, a go/no-go choice involves only one alternative.

- **Open debate.** To generate creative alternatives, you need to facilitate open, constructive debate. Strive to create an environment that supports inquiry-based discussions. Ask open-ended and hypothetical questions to encourage your group to explore a variety of possibilities. Listen attentively to your team's suggestions, and emphasize positive group dynamics. Debate should be task related, not emotional or personal. Make adjustments to your approach if the group is not working well together. Silence and suppressed arguments are both signs that the debate is not sufficiently robust.

- **Assumption testing.** It is unlikely that you will have complete information at the time you make your decision. Your group will have to make assumptions as it proceeds. Make sure that your team recognizes when it is relying on facts and when it is making assumptions. Further, the team needs to recognize which of those assumptions are closely tied to confirmed data, and which are not. The group may still choose to use untested assumptions in its decision-making process, but should reconsider the plausibility of these assumptions throughout the process.

- **Well-defined objectives.** Continually review your objectives during your meetings to ensure that your discussions stay on target. If conditions change, you may need to refine your objectives or even your definition of the problem to meet the new conditions. However, don't let your objectives shift solely because of time pressure or a rush to reach agreement.

- **Perceived fairness.** Keeping people involved throughout the process is critical to the success of your decision. Your team members must feel that their ideas are being considered *during* the process in order to feel a sense of ownership over the final decision. Periodically evaluate the level of participation of your team members, such as after a milestone. If people have stopped participating in conversations or are doing so reluctantly, they may be dissatisfied with the process. Your job is to keep people engaged by acknowledging your team members' suggestions and helping them understand why another alternative may be a better decision.

Paying careful attention to these characteristics throughout the decision-making process can be difficult and time-consuming. Making the effort to include them, however, gives your decision a much better chance of success.

In addition to demonstrating five distinguishing process characteristics, effective decisions are ethical. Let's examine this more closely in the following section.

Making ethical decisions

Whenever you make a decision, particularly a complex one, it will almost certainly affect other people. The consequences will be social as well as economic. Ethics and company values will often be at stake. For example, Radu, a manager of a customer-service phone line at a company that manufactures a new medical monitoring device, has been told that he needs to cut costs. The company is in financial trouble and has to cut costs across the board to stay afloat. Radu's team decides that the alternative that will result in the most savings is to charge customers for phone calls and to reduce the number of hours the line is open. Before making the final decision, however, the group should consider whether that option is a good balance between the interests of the company and those of the customer who may need help using the monitor.

Very few complex decisions can be made on the basis of cost alone. Most decisions involve considering a variety of factors. And these decisions require sound judgment on your part in weighing those factors. As a manager, you need to assess the consequences of your alternatives as best you can and then make a decision.

Ethics should play an important part in your team's deliberations *before* the group makes a decision. Ask your group to explicitly consider ethical issues according to their own values—and not dismiss them as "soft" and therefore unworthy of discussion. For instance, if a team member feels uncomfortable because she heard rumors that the highly successful company you are considering working with overseas has been polluting the environment, she should be encouraged to bring her concerns to the table for deliberation.

One technique to ensure that ethics are considered during your discussions is to appoint an "ethical watchdog," or ombudsman. The person who fills this role would be responsible for ensuring that ethical issues surface during discussions. During the course of the decision-making process, the role of ethical watchdog should rotate periodically.

There is no set of universal guidelines for making ethical decisions. However, a starting point might include asking questions such as "Which option will produce the greatest good and do the least harm?"

At a minimum, make sure that your decision passes the following two tests:

- **The legal test.** The decision is not against the law or against company regulations. For example, it does not discriminate against anyone on the basis of race, gender, age, or religion. You may also want to consider whether something that is technically legal goes against your company's regulations. To illustrate, your company may have a policy that its facilities must comply with all U.S. environmental regulations, even if the facility is located in a country or region where the environmental standards are more relaxed than in the United States.

- **The stakeholder test.** The decision is in the best interest of the company's employees, customers, community, and other key stakeholders, such as federal or state regulators. Sometimes a decision that doesn't directly increase profits is actually in the company's best interest. For instance, a pharmaceutical company's decision to provide low-cost prescriptions to elderly and low-income customers may cost money up front, but it significantly improves the company's brand image, which eventually leads to increased profits in the future.

If your decision passes the two tests above, as a final check, you might want to consider what someone you respect would say if you told them you chose a particular option.

Another key to evaluating the ethics of an option is to consider whether the decision-making and implementation process is open and direct. If you find yourself uncomfortable with the idea that other people will know about the decision, you may *not* be making the ethical choice.

Some companies develop statements about their values and ethical principles. These statements may include goals such as providing top-quality products, reducing waste to the environment, and fostering an open, honest, and direct corporate culture. While you can refer to the company's value statement for guidance, it is unlikely that this document will be enough. You will probably have to use your personal judgment as well.

For example, suppose you have to decide what to do about an employee who has a drug problem. In this case, you may decide that the cost of getting help for this person (e.g., lost time on the job) is outweighed by the value of this person's skills or expertise to your group and your company.

In sum, important decisions cannot be based on financial considerations alone. As a manager, you need to consider the wider ethical dimensions of the decision. That means weighing the consequences of a decision in the broader context of the law, as well as the individuals and community it will affect.

Tips and Tools

Tools for Making Decisions

Setting the Stage

Use this worksheet to think through how you will approach the decision-making process.

Description of Decision

Describe a decision that you and your group needs to make:

Participants

List the names and roles of the people you will include in your decision-making group. Identify key stakeholders, experts, and opponents (individuals who may oppose the decision or block its implementation).

Time

How much time is available to make this decision? Does the decision need to be made by a specific date?

Setting

Where will you meet? (If possible, consider using a location that is different from your usual meeting place.)

Decision-Making Approach

Which approach will you use to make the decision: consensus, majority vote, qualified consensus, directive leadership, or a combination? (Consider the importance and implications of the decision. You may need to reserve the final decision for yourself.) How will you make the choice if the group reaches an impasse?

Climate

List some questions you might ask to encourage debate:

Anticipate some positions on the proposed courses of action that are up for decision.

How will you strike a balance between advocacy- and inquiry-based debate?

Brainstorming Planning

*Use this worksheet to prepare for a brainstorming session. Consider the
parameters for planning the meeting carefully.*

Description of issue/problem:	Date of session:
Who needs to attend:	Why? Special knowledge/skills they contribute?

Materials needed, including:

☐ Flip chart, markers
☐ Easel
☐ Masking tape
☐ Small notes with a sticky backing

☐ Equipment
☐ Visuals
☐ Information handouts
☐ Other:

Session planning:

☐ Opening, warm-up activity
☐ Structured or unstructured brainstorming process
☐ Who will act as recorder
☐ After the session, who will follow up and report to the group
☐ Opposing views to anticipate

Ground rules: For best results, remember to . . .

1. Limit the group's size to between 5 and 15 (though any size group can brainstorm).
2. Assign a neutral facilitator to guide the session.
3. Explain to the group that position and rank play no role during the session.
4. Explain that "reality testing" and forming judgments are not part of the brainstorming session. (All ideas and answers are to be accepted without dispute, criticism, or correction.)
5. Write the problem/issue to brainstorm on a chalkboard or flip chart where everyone can see it throughout the session.
6. Seek agreement from everyone that the issue is stated correctly and precisely.
7. On the chalkboard or flip chart, record all ideas. (Or members may call out ideas, then write them on notes and stick them on the idea board.)
8. Sort the ideas and answers into categories or general groupings. (The group may then sort through and rate or rank order ideas.)
9. After the session, summarize the brainstorming outcomes; report findings to all participants in the group.

Evaluating Alternatives

Use this tool to help you think through your alternatives.

Defining Alternatives

Describe the decision you are trying to make.
Step back and be sure that you are thinking about the root cause of the problem.

List the decision-making objectives your group identified. What criteria will you use to judge success?
Be specific about your goals and quantify wherever possible.

What are some of the most promising alternatives your team explored?
Remember to consider blending alternatives into better solutions.

Evaluating Your Alternatives

For each of the alternatives listed above, write down the factors that are important to consider when making your decision. These factors include:

- **Costs:** How much will the alternative cost? Will it result in cost savings now or over the long term? Are there any hidden costs? Are there likely to be additional costs down the road? Does this alternative meet budget constraints?

- **Benefits:** What kind of profits will we realize if we implement this alternative? Will it increase the quality of our product? Will customer satisfaction increase?

- **Intangibles:** Will our reputation improve if we implement this alternative? Will our customers and/or employees be more loyal?

- **Time:** How long will it take to implement this alternative? Could there be delays? If so, what impact will this have on any schedules?

- **Feasibility:** Can this alternative be implemented realistically? Are there any obstacles that must be overcome? If this alternative is implemented, what resistance might be encountered inside or outside of the organization?

- **Resources:** How many people are needed to implement this alternative? Are they available? What other projects will suffer if individuals focus on this option?

- **Risks:** What are the risks associated with this alternative? For example, could this option result in loss of profits or competitive advantage? Will competitors respond? If so, how?

- **Ethics:** Is this alternative legal? Is it in the best interests of the customers, the employees, and the community where we operate? Would I feel comfortable if other people knew about this alternative?

Alternative 1:

Relevant factors:

Alternative 2:

Relevant factors:

Alternative 3:

Relevant factors:

Communications Notification Form

Once you make a decision, you need to communicate it to those responsible for implementing it and to everyone affected by it. Use this form to keep track of the people you need to inform and to outline what you plan to tell them.

Part I. Who needs to be informed of the decision that's been made?

Those Responsible for Implementation

Name and title	Date to be informed and method	Tasks to be assigned, if applicable
Example: *Janet Doe, Product Manager*	*In-person meeting to review market study and proposed products by 12/1*	*Janet Doe's team to develop plan for new products*

Other Stakeholders and Department Heads

Name and title	Date to be informed and method	Tasks to be assigned, if applicable
Example: *Jonathan Smith, Director, Product Management*	*E-mail John before 12/1 to let him know you will be working with Janet Doe and her team*	*None*

External Constituents and Customers		
Name and title	**Date to be informed and method**	**Tasks to be assigned, if applicable**
Example: Reseller Network	*Send out new-product announcement and collateral before 2/15*	*Identify any seller concerns*

Part II. What needs to be communicated about the decision that's been made?

1. Describe the issue or circumstances that required a decision. Think about this from your stakeholders' perspective.

2. List your objectives, or desired outcomes, in making the decision.

3. List the participants who were involved in making the decision.

4. Briefly explain some of the alternatives that were considered.

5. Discuss the final decision that was reached and its benefit to the stakeholder.

6. Outline the implementation plan and time frame.

7. Recognize those who were involved in the decision-making process.

8. Solicit feedback and comments on the outcome.

Assessing the Decision-Making Process

*Use this tool to assess how well you and your team support
an effective decision-making process.*

Questions about yourself	Rating		
	All of the Time	Some of the Time	Never
1. Do you make sure that the group's objectives in the decision making are clear from the start?			
2. Do you seek out information from a variety of people and sources to make decisions?			
3. Do you frame issues in a way that encourages the exploration of multiple solutions?			
4. Do you make sure that at least one minority viewpoint is considered in all group discussions?			
5. Do you use reliable data and statistics to support your arguments?			
6. Do you involve knowledgeable outsiders to participate in group discussions to provide insight?			
7. Do you encourage team members to step out of their traditional roles when generating alternatives?			
8. Do you facilitate open, constructive dialogue?			
9. Do you ask probing, open-ended questions to promote understanding and the creation of new alternatives?			
10. Do you continually review your objectives during your meetings to ensure that your discussions are on target?			

Questions about your group	Rating		
	All of the Time	**Some of the Time**	**Never**
11. Does everyone in the group participate?			
12. Do group members listen attentively to the viewpoints of others?			
13. Do group members act more like unbiased critical thinkers than advocates of particular interests?			
14. Does your group consider multiple alternatives for a decision?			
15. Does your group take time to ask questions and debate options before coming to agreement?			

Ideas for Improvement

On the basis of your answers, what changes could you make to your decision making to make it more effective? To your group's?

Test Yourself

This section offers ten multiple-choice questions to help you identify your baseline knowledge of decision-making essentials. Answers to the questions are given at the end of the test.

1. Which of the following approaches is likely to lead to excessive group harmony?

   a. Suggest a possible solution in an early meeting to get the group to consider a new idea.

   b. Use the point-counterpoint technique in an early meeting to encourage debate.

   c. Ask someone in an early meeting who hasn't yet participated to make a comment or suggestion.

2. Which of the following is a sign that your discussions may have deteriorated into advocacy mode?

   a. A team member is asking a lot of probing questions of her colleagues at every meeting.

   b. Participants are explaining their viewpoints to each other in the hallways before and after meetings.

   c. The minority viewpoint has generated a lot of conversation during meetings.

3. Which of the following teams would you assemble to choose a new software program to manage the inventory at your warehouse?

    a. Four people from purchasing, five information technology professionals, a warehouse floor supervisor, and a person from finance.

    b. Two people from purchasing, three information technology professionals, and a warehouse floor supervisor.

    c. Three people from purchasing and three information technology professionals.

4. Decide whether the following statement is true or false: creating a decision tree will identify the *best* choice for your problem.

    a. True.

    b. False.

5. Which of the following illustrates an *incorrect* way to facilitate a brainstorming session?

    a. Encourage participants to verbalize any ideas that come into their heads. Record their ideas on a flip chart for evaluation in a follow-up meeting.

    b. At the start of the meeting, ask participants to write down any ideas that come into their heads. Ask them to then share their ideas publicly. As they speak, write down their ideas on a flip chart.

    c. Encourage participants to verbalize any ideas that come into their heads. Discuss the merits of each idea with the group, and record the best ideas on a flip chart.

6. You want to outsource the manufacturing of a printed circuit board. Who is the best person to approach for initial advice?

a. A manager in another department who recently decided to keep manufacturing in-house.

b. A manager in another department who recently started to outsource its manufacturing.

c. A manager in another department who recently mentioned that she thinks outsourcing makes good financial sense.

7. Which of the following is the *best* way to frame an issue related to a high volume of customer complaints about a product?

a. "How can we change the product to increase customer satisfaction?"

b. "What is wrong with the product?"

c. "Why are customers dissatisfied?"

8. Which of the following is an example of the point-counter-point approach to decision making?

a. A manager asks each team member to come to a meeting prepared to present his or her ideas to the other group members. The group then discusses each proposal and tries to find a set of assumptions and recommendations that the group can accept.

b. A manager asks half of the group to come to a meeting prepared to present a proposal they created together to the other group members. The other half of the group critiques the proposal and presents its analysis. The whole group then tries to find a set of assumptions and recommendations that the group can accept.

c. A manager splits his team into two subgroups. He asks one subgroup to come to a meeting prepared to present a proposal; he asks the other subgroup to be prepared to present an opposing proposal. After both presentations have been made, the whole group tries to agree on a course of action.

9. Once you make a decision, what should you do next?

a. Assign reasonable and attainable tasks to your team and to anyone else who will need to implement the decision.

b. Create a work plan that outlines the tasks you will take to implement your decision.

c. Identify who should know about the decision.

10. Decide whether the following statement is true or false: if a decision is legal and maximizes profits, then it is an ethical course of action.

a. True.

b. False.

Answers to test questions

1, a. If you, as a manager, make a suggestion early in a meeting in the hopes of encouraging your team to consider other alternatives, your action can backfire. Employees may view the suggestion as your preferred solution and support the idea to try to please you. To avoid excessive group harmony, consider using a technique that encourages people to consider multiple options and to critique each other, such as point-counterpoint. Also encourage those individuals who are reluctant to participate to voice their opinions.

2, b. In an advocacy-based discussion, people try to persuade each other to support their viewpoints. Team members who are discussing their views in the hallway may be trying to convince others of the merits of their ideas. These individuals could influence others to see the decision process in terms of winners and losers—which doesn't lead to good decision making. On the other hand, if your team is asking probing questions and considering minority viewpoints, it is adopting the more inquiry-based approach essential to effective business decisions.

3, b. This group contains representatives from departments that will be affected by the change, and the team is a reasonable size. Unless you need a bigger group to accommodate a variety of perspectives, aim for five to seven participants in a decision-making team. Larger groups are more difficult to manage.

4, b. A decision tree will *not* necessarily point to the best solution. Instead, it provides a visual representation of the uncertainties and possible outcomes associated with a decision. Thus, it helps you evaluate your options. You will still need to assess the information in the decision tree to make your choice. Creating a prioritization matrix may help you evaluate your options at this stage.

5, c. Discussing the merits of each idea as it is offered will probably *not* encourage brainstorming, because brainstorming should be used to generate alternatives—not to evaluate them as they're presented. When leading a brainstorming session, ask people to focus on identifying as many alternatives as possible rather than criticizing or debating ideas as they're presented. You can evaluate ideas later, after you've generated an exhaustive list of options.

6, a. A common mistake people make when considering a decision is to seek information that supports their existing point of view and to ignore information that contradicts it. When faced with a decision, asking a colleague to argue against your potential decision may identify weaknesses that you haven't yet considered. Seeking only people who have similar views or who have made a similar decision is likely to strengthen your resolve to proceed without sufficiently careful consideration.

7, c. When trying to frame an issue, it's good to ask questions that encourage exploration and to avoid questions that assume the nature of the problem (such as "How can we change the product?" or "What's wrong with the product?"). Your goal is to get at the core of the issue before you begin examining possible solutions.

8, c. To use the point-counterpoint technique, you divide your team into two groups and ask them to develop opposing proposals. After both groups present their proposals, the whole group tries to agree on a course of action. The point-counterpoint technique—as well as a consensus approach and the intellectual-watchdog technique described in the other options—are all useful for encouraging team members to reach a final decision.

9, c. Once you make a decision, you need to determine who should know about it. You do not want to start implementing a decision until you are sure that the people who will be affected by the decision are aware of your plans. A common mistake is to make a decision with a team of people and then forget to inform others of the course of action that was chosen. While other people may not be directly involved in implementing your decision, they may still be affected by it.

10, b. Even though a decision may be legal, it is not necessarily the right thing to do. As a manager, you have a responsibility to consider ethics when making a decision. Your personal values and any corporate statements of social responsibility will guide you. Ultimately, you must balance the interests of all stakeholders, from those who will gain from a decision to those who could be adversely affected.

To Learn More

Articles

Bagley, Constance E. "The Ethical Leader's Decision Tree." *Harvard Business Review*, February 2003.

If you spring for optional pollution-control devices at your overseas plant, have you violated your duty to maximize shareholder value? This article provides a framework for exposing conflicts between corporate actions and corporate ethics that can help clarify ethical dilemmas—and potentially head off bad decisions.

Charan, Ram. "Conquering a Culture of Indecision." *Harvard Business Review* OnPoint Enhanced Edition, April 2002.

The single greatest cause of corporate underperformance is the failure to execute. Author Ram Charan, drawing on a quarter century of observing organizational behavior, perceives that such failures are caused by a misfire in the personal interactions that are supposed to produce results. The inability to take decisive action is rooted in a company's culture. But, Charan notes, since leaders create a culture of indecisiveness, they can also break it. This article provides guidance for leaders to move their organizations from paralysis to action.

Garvin, David, and Michael Roberto. "What You Don't Know About Making Decisions." *Harvard Business Review* OnPoint Enhanced Edition, November 2003.

The authors take a closer look at inquiry—a highly productive decision-making approach. When you balance advocacy with inquiry, you carefully consider a variety of options, work with others to discover the best solutions, and stimulate creative thinking rather than suppressing dissension. The payoff? High-quality decisions that advance your company's objectives and that you reach in a timely manner and implement effectively. But inquiry isn't easy. Garvin and Roberto explain how to manage the three keys to using inquiry: promoting constructive conflict, accepting ambiguity, and balancing *divergence* during early discussions with *unity* during implementation of the decision.

Hammond, John S., Ralph L. Keeney, and Howard Raiffa. "The Hidden Traps in Decision Making." *Harvard Business Review* OnPoint Enhanced Edition, November 2000.

The human mind is prone to distortions and biases that can undermine even the most well-thought-out decision-making process. This article examines eight psychological traps that are particularly likely to affect the way we make business decisions. The best way to avoid these traps is awareness—forewarned is forearmed. The authors also show executives how to take other simple steps to protect themselves and their organizations from various kinds of mental lapses.

Kim, W. Chan, and Renée A. Mauborgne, "Fair Process: Managing in the Knowledge Economy." *Harvard Business Review* OnPoint Enhanced Edition, February 2000.

Unlike the traditional factors of production—land, labor, and capital—knowledge is a resource that can't be forced out of people. But creating and sharing knowledge is essential to fostering innovation, the key challenge of the knowledge-based economy. To create a climate in which employees volunteer their creativity and expertise, managers need to look beyond the traditional tools at their disposal. They need to build trust. The authors have studied the links between trust, idea sharing, and corporate performance for more than a decade. They offer an explanation for why people resist change even when it would benefit them directly. In every case, the decisive factor was what the authors call fair process—fairness in the way a company makes and executes decisions. Fair process may sound like a soft issue, but it is crucial to building trust and unlocking ideas.

Luecke, Richard. "Make Better Decisions." *Harvard Management Update*, April 2006.

We know that individuals can be trained to make better decisions, but as greater authority is moved into the hands of frontline managers, developing a broadly based decision competency is becoming more important. Some corporations are taking steps to enhance organizational decision competence. Learn how two of these companies, General Motors and Chevron, developed programs for improving decision quality and how they got started.

Rogers, Paul, and Marcia Blenko. "Who Has the D? How Clear Decision Roles Enhance Organizational Performance." *Harvard Business Review* OnPoint Enhanced Edition, January 2006.

Decisions are the coin of the realm in business. But even in highly respected companies, decisions can get stuck inside the organization like loose change. As a result, the entire decision-making process can stall, usually at one of four bottlenecks: global versus local, center versus business unit, function versus function, and inside versus outside partners. Decision-making bottlenecks can occur whenever there is ambiguity or tension over who gets to decide what. For example, do marketers or product developers get to decide the features of a new product? Should a major capital investment depend on the approval of the business unit that will own it, or should headquarters make the final call? Bain consultants Paul Rogers and Marcia Blenko use an approach called RAPID (recommend, agree, perform, input, and decide) to help companies unclog their decision-making bottlenecks by explicitly defining roles and responsibilities. When revamping its decision-making process, a company must take some practical steps: align decision roles with the most important sources of value, make sure that decisions are made by the right people at the right levels of the organization, and let the people who will live with the new process help design it.

Books

Bazerman, Max H. *Judgment in Managerial Decision Making.* New York: John Wiley & Sons, 2002.

In situations requiring careful judgment, we're all influenced by our own biases. Bazerman's book provides a framework to help managers overcome those biases to make better decisions. Through the use of vivid real-world examples, Bazerman identifies systematic ways in which judgment and decision-making skills deviate from rationality under uncertain conditions. The book provides practical strategies and exercises for changing and improving your decision-making processes so they become part of your permanent behavior.

Garvin, David A. *General Management: Processes and Action*. Boston: McGraw-Hill, 2002.

Understanding the skills necessary to influence the design, direction, and functioning of management processes is essential to effective management. Focusing on implementation and the way general managers get things done, Garvin walks through management processes like strategic planning, business planning, decision making, and budgeting to help move an organization forward. Using real-world examples, Garvin illustrates a wide range of management processes and activities and their link to performance.

Janis, Irving L. *Victims of Groupthink*. Boston: Houghton Mifflin, 1972.

Using examples drawn from the American government, Janis tests his hypothesis that groups often tend to make more extreme decisions than individuals. From the Bay of Pigs invasion to the Watergate cover-up, Janis portrays in detail how group dynamics helped to put participants on a disastrous course and keep them there. In addition, Janis presents fresh ideas on how and why groupthink occurs, and offers suggestions for avoiding it.

eLearning Programs

Harvard Business School Publishing. *Case in Point*. Boston: Harvard Business School Publishing, 2004.

Case in Point is a flexible set of online cases, designed to help prepare middle- and senior-level managers for a variety of leadership challenges. These short, reality-based scenarios provide sophisticated content to create a focused view into the realities of the life of a leader. Your managers will experience Aligning Strategy, Removing Implementation Barriers, Overseeing Change, Anticipating Risk, Ethical Decisions, Building a Business Case, Cultivating Customer Loyalty, Emotional Intelligence, Developing a Global Perspective, Fostering Innovation, Defining Problems, Selecting Solutions, Managing Difficult Interactions, The Coach's Role, Delegating for Growth, Managing Creativity, Influencing Others, Managing Performance, Providing Feedback, and Retaining Talent.

Harvard Business School Publishing. *Decision Making*. Boston: Harvard Business School Publishing, 2002.

Based on research and writings of leadership experts, this program examines the frameworks for making decisions, decision-making biases, and the role of intuition in this context. Increase the decision-making confidence in an organization by equipping managers with the interactive lessons, expert guidance, and activities for immediate application at work. Managers will learn to recognize the role intuition plays in decision making, apply a process to complicated decisions, identify and avoid thinking traps, simplify complex decisions, and tackle fast decision making.

Harvard Business School Publishing. *Managing Difficult Conversations*. Boston: Harvard Business School Publishing, 2001.

This program will help you understand why disagreements occur and help you build conclusions collaboratively. These productive dialogue skills will lead to a more accurate, shared understanding of the information exchanged in your daily interactions. *Managing Difficult Conversations* examines techniques for approaching and handling difficult business conversations. The program explores how mental models influence our private thinking and, thus, our behavior. It presents the Left-Hand Column exercise as a technique for unveiling and examining our internal thought process. The program also examines five unproductive thinking habits that many people fall into during difficult conversations and five productive alternative ways of thinking. By examining your own thinking habits and actively seeking more productive mind-sets, you can learn to approach difficult conversations with confidence, avoid blaming, overcome defensiveness, and make better business decisions.

Harvard Business School Publishing. *Productive Business Dialogue*. Boston: Harvard Business School Publishing, 2002.

This program shows managers how to craft conversations that are fact based, minimize defensiveness, and draw out the best thinking from everyone involved. *Productive Business Dialogue* introduces the Ladder of Inference, a tool that helps participants in a dialogue understand the distinctions among fact, interpretation, and conclusions and how making these distinctions clear can dramatically enhance the productivity of meetings and discussions. Through interactive, real-world scenarios, you will practice shaping interactions that maximize learning and lead to better-informed decisions.

Sources for Making Decisions

The following sources aided in development of this book:

Bagley, Constance E. "The Ethical Leader's Decision Tree." *Harvard Business Review*, February 2003.

Bazerman, Max H. *Judgment in Managerial Decision Making.* New York: John Wiley & Sons, 2002.

Cadbury, Sir Adrian. "Ethical Managers Make Their Own Rules." *Harvard Business Review*, September–October 1987.

Charan, Ram. "Conquering a Culture of Indecision." *Harvard Business Review*, April 2001.

Crowe, Mattison. "Why the Members of Your Team Won't Speak Up, and What You Can Do About It." *Harvard Management Update*, November 1996.

Drucker, Peter F. "The Effective Decision." *Harvard Business Review*, January–February 1967.

Garvin, David A. *General Management: Processes and Action.* Boston: McGraw-Hill, 2002.

Garvin, David A., and Michael A. Roberto. "What You Don't Know About Making Decisions." *Harvard Business Review* OnPoint Enhanced Edition, September 2001.

Gary, Loren. "Cognitive Bias: Systemic Errors in Decision Making." *Harvard Management Update*, April 1998.

Gary, Loren. "Problem Solving for Decision Makers." *Harvard Management Update*, December 1997.

Hammond, John S., Ralph L. Keeney, and Howard Raiffa. "Even Swaps: A Rational Method for Making Trade-offs." *Harvard Business Review*, March–April 1998.

Hammond, John S., Ralph L. Keeney, and Howard Raiffa. "The Hidden Traps in Decision Making." *Harvard Business Review*, September–October 1998.

Janis, Irving L. *Victims of Groupthink*. Boston: Houghton Mifflin, 1972.

Kim, W. Chan, and Renée A. Mauborgne. "Fair Process: Managing in the Knowledge Economy." *Harvard Business Review*, February 2000.

Magee, John F. "Decision Trees for Decision Making." *Harvard Business Review*, July–August 1964.

Morgan, Nick. "Put Your Decision Making to the Test: Communicate." *Harvard Management Communication Letter*, November 2001.

Straus, David, and Pat Milton. "Collaborative Decision Making." *Development*, July 2003.

Notes

How to Order

Harvard Business Press publications are available worldwide from your local bookseller or online retailer.

You can also call:
1-800-668-6780

Our product consultants are available to help you 8:00 a.m.–6:00 p.m., Monday–Friday, Eastern Time. Outside the U.S. and Canada, call: 617-783-7450.

Please call about special discounts for quantities greater than ten.

You can order online at:
www.HBSPress.org